PIED BEAUTY

Poem by Gerard Manley Hopkins

Illustrations and commentary by Glencora Pipkin

THIS PROJECT IS DEDICATED TO MY
GRANDMOTHER LOUISE WHO TAUGHT ME NOT
ONLY TO LOVE GOOD POETRY BUT TO SPREAD IT
THROUGHOUT THE WORLD.

Something that is dappled has many spots that are colored differently from the background color.

A leopard is dappled and so is a fawn.
Can you think of an animal that is dappled?

Another word for dappled could be freckled.
Do you have freckles?

Glory be to God for

DAPPLED *things*

The word brinded refers to a pattern of a brownish or greyish color with many streaks of different colors throughout.

How many colors can you see in the morning sky?
What about in the evening sky?

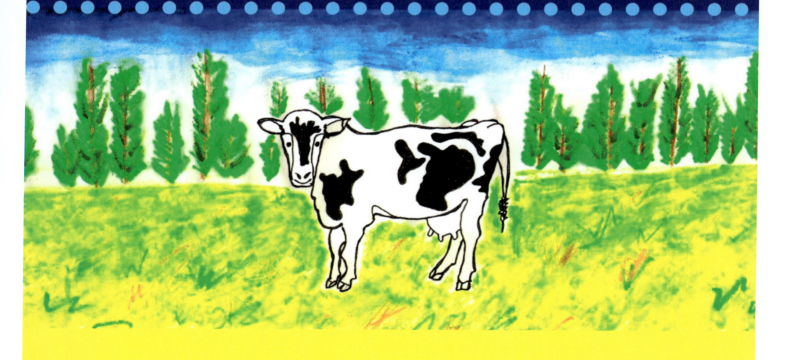

Trout are a freshwater fish, and they have many different colorations.

Some trout have rose-colored tiny spots, or stipples, on their scales.

Their coloring is a kind of camouflage. This means their coloring will change when they change habitats.

A finch is a small bird, and its wings are often speckled, striped, or patterned. Because birds are so small (and they move so quickly!), it's often hard to see such tiny detail.

Next time you see a bird, try to focus on just the bird's wings. Are they different colored than its body?Do you see any patterns like stripes or dots?

A landscape can be used for many different purposes. Two of those purposes are for harvesting vegetables and for letting animals, such as sheep, graze. Sometimes fields are left empty, which are called "fallow."

When sheep are fenced in a field, they are called part of the "fold." This is where shepherds take special care to watch them.

As for fields for harvesting, the land is ploughed which turns up the topsoil and makes the soil ready for planting.

A trade is the work that someone does. A plumber is in the the trade of plumbing, and a teacher is in the trade of teaching.

What kind of gear, or tools, do you use? What gear does a fisher use? A mechanic? A mom? A dad?

The animals pictured here are the narwhal (top), the platypus, the bearded lizard, and the armadillo (bottom left to right).

These animals are counter, original, spare and strange.

Have you ever seen one of these animals?
Can you name another strange animal?

The moon is often called "fickle" because its shape changes in the sky during the month. During a month's cycle, the moon goes from waxing (becoming full) to waning (becoming empty).

This line focuses on opposites:

swift & slow

sweet & sour

adazzle & dim

Can you think of things that are both sweet and sour?

With swift, slow;
  sweet, sour;
    adazzle, dim;

God has created all things on this earth, and many of his created objects are changing constantly. However, God and His love do not change.

Praise Him

Printed in Great Britain
by Amazon